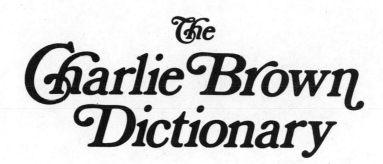

The Charlie Brown Dictionary

by Charles M. Schulz

Based on THE RAINBOW DICTIONARY
by Wendell W. Wright, Ph.D.,
assisted by Helene Laird.

WORLD PUBLISHING
TIMES MIRROR
NEW YORK

An Explanation

This volume is the seventh in a series of eight books which together form a complete, easy-to-handle dictionary for children using the characters from *Peanuts,* probably the most popular comic strip ever to appear.

Charlie Brown himself, Snoopy wearing his dish as a hat, Linus with his security blanket, Lucy giving advice, all help to motivate children to learn about the hundreds of words defined in this volume.

A complete explanation about this dictionary, including the lists from which the entries were chosen, the methods used to present definitions and the many ways in which this book can be helpful, is found in the introduction to the first volume. If you have already used the first volume, you will find that the same high standards for word selections and definitions prevail here.

The activities, situations, thoughts and conversation of the *Peanuts* characters will hold the child's interest while he continues to increase his vocabulary and his comprehension. As he goes through this book and the others that complete *The Charlie Brown Dictionary,* he will be having a vital learning experience that is also joyful, and the happiness will make the knowledge he gains that much more meaningful.

Published by The World Publishing Company
Published simultaneously in Canada
by Nelson, Foster & Scott Ltd.
First printing—1973
Illustrations, Copyright © 1973 by United
Feature Syndicate, Inc. Peanuts cartoons.
Copyright © 1959, 1960, 1961, 1962, 1963, 1964,
1965, 1966, 1967, 1968, 1969, 1970, 1971
by United Feature Syndicate.

Text, Copyright © 1973 by The World Publishing Company.
Previous edition, THE RAINBOW DICTIONARY,
Copyright © 1947, 1959 by The World Publishing Company.

Acknowledgment is made to Lee Mendelson—
Bill Melendez TV Productions,
for illustrations from the television productions,
It's The Great Pumpkin, Charlie Brown;
"He's Your Dog, Charlie Brown!";
"You're In Love, Charlie Brown";
It Was A Short Summer, Charlie Brown;
Play It Again, Charlie Brown; and Charlie Brown's All-Stars,
all by Charles M. Schulz and
published by The World Publishing Company.
Acknowledgement is also made to George O'Hara,
acquiring editor, for enthusiastic support in this project.

Library of Congress Catalog Card Number: 72-12135
ISBN 0-529-04463-3 (Trade Edition)
ISBN 0-529-05088-9 (Library Edition)
Printed in The United States of America.

WORLD PUBLISHING
TIMES MIRROR

step   **Step** to the back of the bus.
Walk to the back of the bus.

I **stepped** around the puddle.

---

stepladder   A **stepladder** is a **short ladder** with three or four steps.   Stepladders stand on four legs.

---

stew   Sometimes we have **stew** for dinner.   Stew is made of meat, potatoes, and vegetables.   It is cooked slowly on the top of the stove.

---

stewardess   The **stewardess** on an airplane helps take care of the passengers.   She wears a pretty uniform. The stewardess brings the people on the plane things to eat and drink.

---

stick   Charlie Brown is holding a **stick**.
He is holding a **long thin piece of wood**.

Don't **stick** your hand with the pin.
Don't **put the sharp point** of the pin in your hand.

Stick the stamp on the letter.
Fasten the stamp on the letter.

The car got **stuck** in the mud.

sticky   Paint that is almost dry—but is not completely dry—
is **sticky.**   If you touch it with your finger, you cannot
easily pull your finger away from it.   The paint seems
to hold your finger.

---

stiff   My new shoes feel **stiff.**   They **do not bend easily** when I
walk.

---

still   Snoopy had been barking.   Then he became **still.**
He **didn't make any noise.**

He curled up and lay **still.**
He curled up and lay **without moving.**

Snoopy **still** hasn't moved.
Snoopy hasn't moved **up to now.**

---

sting   Did a bee ever **sting** you?   It feels as though you are
being stuck with a pin.

Lucy was **stung** on the arm by a bee.   Her arm hurt
and swelled up.

---

stir   I must **stir** the soup.
I must **move** the soup **round and round with my spoon.**

---

stitch   If you can sew, you can make a **stitch.**   When your needle
and thread go in one place and come out at another
place, you have made a **stitch.**   A stitch connects the
two pieces of cloth you are sewing together.

stocking   Sally is going to hang up
her **stocking.**   Stockings
are longer than socks.
They cover our legs
and feet.

Mother has a pair of black stockings.

---

stomach

Snoopy ran head first into
Charlie Brown's
stomach.   He hit
Charlie Brown right
in the **middle of his
body.**

When you swallow food, it goes down your
throat into your stomach.

---

stone   A **stone** is a **piece of rock.**   Linus threw a stone
into the air.

My mother's ring has a **stone** in it.   The stone is a
diamond.

---

stool   A **chair without a back** is a **stool.**   We use it in the
kitchen to sit on.   The farmer uses a stool to sit
on while he milks the cows.

stop Charlie Brown is waiting for the bus to **stop.**
He is waiting for the bus to **arrive.**
He waited so long he fell asleep.

The red light on the street means **"Stop!"**
The red light on the street means **"Do not go any farther."**

"Please **stop** shouting," Mother said.   **"Don't do it any more."**

I **stopped** my dog from following me down the street.
The light is red, so the cars are **stopping.**

stoop Linus had to **stoop** to pick the stone from the ground.
He had to **bend** his body **forward** and down so that he
can get hold of the stone.

A **stoop** is what we call a few stairs in front of a house.
We sit on our stoop when the weather is hot.

store A **place where things are sold** is a **store.**   We buy our
food in a grocery store.

The farmer will **store** the corn for his pigs to eat during
the winter.

The farmer will **put away** the corn for his pigs to eat
during the winter.

In the summer, my mother **stores** my winter clothes
in a closet.

---

storm

Lucy and Snoopy are out in a
storm.   The wind is blowing
hard and the rain is pouring down.
Sometimes thunder and
lightning come with a storm.

The snow is falling thick and fast.
We are having a snowstorm.

---

story Aunt Ellen is telling a **story.**   The story is
"The Three Bears."

---

stove Mother cooks on a **stove** in the kitchen.   In some houses,
there is a stove to warm the rooms.

---

straight I tried to draw a **straight** line.
I tried to draw a line with no bumps or bends in it.
But it came out a little bit crooked.

strange   I will start tomorrow at a **strange** school.   I have never
been there before.

I will be in a class with strange children.   I don't
know any of them.

A dragon is a **strange**-looking animal.
A dragon is a **queer**-looking animal.

---

straw   Linus is drinking through a **straw.**
A straw is usually made of paper.
It is hollow, and you can pull water
through it with your breath.

The **dry, hollow stems** of the wheat
plant that are left after the grains
are taken are also called **straw.**

I have a straw hat.

---

stream   Snoopy is crossing the **stream** by stepping on stones.
A stream is **a little river.**

Something that moves in a straight,
narrow line is sometimes called
a stream.
A stream of cars sped by.
The light streamed in the window.

---

street   A **street** is a **road in the city or town.**   The street I
live on is called Main Street.   What is the name of
your street?   There are many streets in our town.

strength "I have the **strength** of a lion,"
says Charlie Brown.
"I am **strong** enough to carry
two more bundles."

stretch "See how high I can **stretch**." Linus is showing
Charlie Brown how high he **can reach out his arms.**

I **stretch** a rubber band.
I **pull out** the rubber band so that
it is longer.

Linus **stretched** to catch the ball.
I am **stretching** my sweater to make it bigger.

strike I saw Lucy **strike** her
little brother.
I saw her **hit** him **hard.**

When you play baseball,
you try to hit the
ball with your
baseball bat. If you
miss the ball when
you try to hit it, that
is called a **strike.**
If you miss the ball three times,
you have **struck out.**

When Lucy **struck** him, Linus fell on his head.
Striking someone is a dangerous thing to do.

string   We use **string** to tie packages.   When you buy string
in the store, it is rolled into a ball.

strip   My belt is made of a **strip** of leather.
My belt is made of a **narrow piece** of leather.

He will **strip** and jump into the water.
He will **take off his clothes** and jump into the water.

stripe   A **stripe** is a narrow line of color
with different colors on each side
of it.
Daddy has a tie with red, blue and
yellow stripes.
He has a blue and white striped shirt too.
Linus always wears **a shirt with red and black stripes.**

strong   A **strong** man can lift heavy things.   He is **not weak.**

When I read, I like a strong light so that I can see well.

Our big swing hangs from a strong rope.

Some kinds of cheese have a strong taste.

stuff   Daddy said, "I don't need the **stuff** in that box."
Daddy said, "I don't need the **things** in that box."

When I make my bear, I will **stuff** it with cotton.
When I make my bear, I will **fill** it with cotton.

My bed pillow is **stuffed** with feathers.

such I have read several **such** books.
I have read several books **of that kind.**

He was **such** a big dog!
He was **a very** big dog!

---

sugar **Sugar** is made from a plant called sugar cane.   It is also made from sugar beets.   I sweeten my lemonade with sugar.   There is sugar in candy.   Sugar makes the candy sweet.

---

suit

Did you ever see a dog wearing a **suit?**
Snoopy is wearing a **jacket and trousers that match.**

Charlie Brown and Sally are going swimming.   They wear **bathing suits.**

This hat **suits me.**
This hat **looks good on me.**

I hope this book will **suit** you.   I hope it will **please** you.

---

suitcase A **suitcase** is a **bag** used **for carrying clothes** when you travel.   Snoopy also puts his dish in his suitcase when he goes on a trip.

---

summer The **summer** is one of the four **seasons** of the year. The other seasons are autumn, winter and spring. There is much sunshine in the summer.   The sunshine makes summer a warm season.

Ss

sun

The **sun** shines in the daytime.
It is bright and makes you warm.

Sunday **Sunday** is the first **day** of the week.   Most people do
not go to work on Sunday.   Sunday is a day of rest.
Many people go to church on Sunday.

sunshine The **light of the sun** is **sunshine**.   Plants grow in the
sunshine.   Sunshine is good for children.

supper Sally is bringing Snoopy
his **supper.**
We eat **supper** in the evening.
We have a **light dinner**
in the evening.

suppose I **suppose** we should go.
I **think perhaps** we should go.

I **supposed** they would be late.
I **guessed** they would be late.

I'm **supposed** to go out today.
I **should** go out today.

Supposing we go tomorrow instead?
How would it be if we went tomorrow instead?

sure I am **sure** that I am eight years old. I am sure that I am a boy. I am sure that my name is Richard Jones. I **know** all these things.

---

surprise

Snoopy got a **surprise**.
He got **something he did not expect.**

Snoopy was **surprised** that he caught the ball.
He **did not expect** to catch it.

---

surround Many trees **surround** our house.
They are **all around** our house.

An island is **surrounded** by water.
There are flowers **surrounding** the pond.

---

swallow When I eat, I chew my food, then I **swallow** it.
It goes down my throat into my stomach.

---

swamp **A wet, muddy piece of land** is called a **swamp.** You will find many birds and plants in swamps.

swap "Let's **swap** dinners," says Snoopy. "You can have my dog food, and I'll have your turkey." To swap is to give someone a thing that you own, and get something back from him in return.

swat Charlie Brown tried to **swat** the mosquito, but he missed. To **swat** is to hit or **slap quickly.**

sway Did you see the branches of the tree **sway** in the wind? Did you see the branches **gently swing from side to side** in the wind?

sweat When the day is hot and you are running fast, you begin to **sweat.** Your **skin becomes damp.**

sweater

Charlie Brown has a new **sweater.** He has a **short jacket made of yarn** to keep him warm.

sweep   I **sweep** the floor.
I **brush** the floor **with a broom** to clean it.

Frieda was **sweeping** the leaves from the walk.
She has **swept** the walk clean.

---

sweet   Sugar is **sweet.**   Anything made with sugar is sweet.
Candy is sweet.   Honey is sweet too.

Mother says, "Baby is so sweet!"

---

swell   To **swell** means to **grow bigger.**   When I blow air into
the balloon, it will swell.   Linus pinched his finger in
the door, and it began to swell.

Sometimes the children say, "That's **swell!**"
They mean, "That's **very good.**"

---

swerve   We saw the **car drive straight** down the road and then
swerve to the right.   We saw it **turn suddenly** to the right.

---

swift   Peppermint Patty is a **swift**
runner.
She is a **very fast** runner.

She is **swifter** than her friends.
She runs **swiftly.**

swim   The girls can **swim** better than the boys.
They **glide** smoothly **through the water.**

They **swam** across the lake quickly.
The boys were **swimming** behind them.

The girls are good swimmers because they have **swum**
     more than the boys.

swing   There is a **swing** in our yard.
I like to sit on it and **swing.**
I like to **move back and forth through the air.**

I saw a monkey **swinging** by his tail.
He **swung** from branch to branch.

sword A **sword** is a long, sharp and pointed **weapon.**   Swords used to be carried by soldiers when they went to war.

syrup When Snoopy eats pancakes, he covers them with **syrup.** Syrup is a **sweet, thick liquid,** made from boiling sugar and water.

T t

table The children are seated around the **table.**   The table has a
flat top held up by strong legs.   They will eat their
dinner at the table.

tablet Schroeder is drawing a picture in his **tablet.** A tablet has many **pages for writing** or drawing. The pages are fastened together at one end. Other words for tablet are **notebook** and **pad.**

table tennis Do you know how to play the **game** called **table tennis?** A player stands at each end of a long green table. The players hold small wooden rackets and try to hit a little white ball across a net with their rackets.

tack A **tack** is a **little nail** with a flat top. Sometimes these tacks are called "thumb tacks," because you push them in with your thumb. When you **tack** something to a wall, you fasten it to the wall with a tack.

tackle What does Snoopy like best about football? He likes to **tackle** Charlie Brown. When you tackle someone, you **catch** him and make him fall or stop running.

tadpole When a frog is very young, it is called a **tadpole.** A tadpole does not look like a frog; it looks like a tiny fish. But soon it grows strong back legs and can jump fast and far.

tag   There was a **tag** on my Christmas present.
There was a **piece of card tied with a string** on my Christmas
present.

There is a **game** called **tag.**   One player runs after another
until he touches him.   Do you know how to play tag?

tail   Dogs and many other animals
have **tails.**   Snoopy wags his
tail when he is happy.
Sometimes he sits on his tail.

tailor   When Marcie tore her coat, her mother took it to a **tailor**
to be fixed.   A tailor is **a person who is paid to sew
clothes.**   Some tailors are able to make dresses and suits.

take      Snoopy doesn't want Lucy to **take**
his supper dish away.
He doesn't want her to **get hold of**
it and **carry** it away.

Daddy will **take** us to the ball game.
Daddy will **go with us** to the ball game.

I will **take** a book from the shelf.
I will **get** a book from the shelf.

I will **take** five minutes to get ready.
I will **need** five minutes to get ready.

406

We **take** a bus to go downtown.
We **ride** on a bus to go downtown.

You **take** the stairs to the second floor.
You **walk** on the stairs to the second floor.

Take this package to Mother.
Carry this package to Mother.

Pig-Pen has **taken** one cookie.
Mother **takes** me to the show.
Linus is **taking** a ride on his sled.

took   Violet **took** her books home with her.

tale   Our kindergarten teacher told us the **tale** of
"Little Red Riding Hood."
Our kindergarten teacher told the **story** of
"Little Red Riding Hood."

talent   Schroeder has a **talent** for
playing the piano.
He is **able** to play the piano
very well.

talk   Charlie Brown and Lucy are having a **talk**.
To **talk** means to **say words**. I can talk to my dog, but my dog cannot talk to me.

I **talked** to Daddy over the telephone.
I was **talking** about the animals I saw at the circus.

---

tall   Linus is **not** very **tall**. He is **short**.

Violet is **taller** than he is. Her head is above his.

Violet is **taller** than the snowman. She is the **tallest** of them all.

---

tame   A **tame** animal is one that is not afraid of people. Dogs and cats and horses are tame animals. Lions and tigers are wild animals. Tame animals are usually **gentle**.

---

tan   Charlie Brown wore tan shoes.
Charlie Brown wore **light brown** shoes.

Lucy played in the sun every day. She got a nice tan.

---

tangerine   A **tangerine** is a **fruit** that looks like a small orange.

tap We heard a **tap** on the window.
We heard a **light knock** on the window.

Will you **tap** that boy on the shoulder?
Will you **touch** that boy on the shoulder?

---

tardy I must not be **tardy** to school.
I must not be **late** to school.

---

target Something that we try to hit with arrows or a toy gun is a
target. Usually a target has several little circles inside
a large circle. We try to hit the little circle in the center
of the target. Because it is the smallest circle, it is
the hardest one to hit.

---

task Snoopy's **task** today is washing the dishes. A task is a
special job that has to be done. Charlie Brown's task is to
feed Snoopy every day. Sally's **work** is to help Snoopy and
Charlie Brown. Franklin's task is to make his bed
every morning.

taste   Sugar has a sweet **taste.**   Lemons have a sour taste.

Baby likes **to taste** any new food before she eats it.
Baby likes **to take a little bite** of any new food before
she eats it.

I **tasted** the cake.   It tasted good.

---

tax   Everybody has to help pay to keep the streets clean.   We all
have to help pay for firemen, policemen and schools.
The money we give to the city or to the country to help
pay for all this is called a **tax.**

---

taxicab   A **taxicab** is a **special automobile** that takes you where
you want to go.   You pay the taxicab driver to
drive you from one place to another.

---

tea   Mother sometimes drinks **tea.**   She makes it by putting leaves
of a tea plant in hot water.   Sometimes she makes it by
putting a tea bag in hot water.

---

teach   **Teach** me to read.
Help me **learn** to read.

taught   Mother **taught** me to write my name.
She says **teaching** me is fun.

teacher   My **teacher** at school helps me learn to read.   My mother
        is my teacher in the kitchen.   She shows me how to cook.

---

team   Charlie Brown and his friends are going to play baseball
        together.   They are a **team.**

A baseball team is made up of nine players.
A football team has eleven players.
A basketball team is made up of five players.

Two horses pulling something **together** are called a **team.**

---

tear   Who would want to **tear** Linus's picture?
        Who would want to **pull** the picture
            apart?

Someone **tore** the picture because he
    didn't like it.
Do you suppose the picture was
    torn by Linus himself?

tear

Charlie Brown is crying. His face is wet with **tears**. A **tear** is a **drop of water** that comes out of your eye when you cry.

tease   We **tease** Sally about the little boy who walks home with her. We **joke with** Sally about the little boy who walks home with her.

I **tease** my mother to let me go to the circus. I **ask** my mother **again and again** to let me go to the circus.

Don't tease the kitten. He doesn't like it.

teddy bear

Lucy got up to get her **teddy bear.** She likes to take her teddy bear to bed with her. He is soft and pretty. Her teddy bear is her favorite **toy.**

telephone   Peppermint Patty is speaking on the **telephone** to someone who is far away. Her voice is carried by a telephone wire to someone who is listening to another telephone at the other end of the wire.

telescope   Have you ever looked through a **telescope**? It makes things that are far away seem much closer.

television   Charlie Brown is watching a show on the **television**
set.   He sees moving pictures of things
happening far away.   He hears people talking
and singing.   Charlie Brown loves to watch **TV**.

tell   Do not **tell** where Mother keeps the cookies.
Do not **say** where Mother keeps the cookies.

Violet **told** Lucy a secret.

temper   Your **temper** is the way you feel.   Lucy has a terrible
temper.   Franklin says, "Keep your temper, Lucy.
Don't shout and fight."

tempt When somebody tries to get you to do something wrong, he may **tempt** you. If you are not supposed to eat candy, he may say, "Oh, have just one little bite." You should not be **tempted,** because the candy might give you a stomach ache. Lucy is trying to tempt Linus to eat some candy.

ten There are **ten** cents in a dime.
There are **10** cents in a dime.

Let's count to **ten:**
1 2 3 4 5 6 7 8 9 **10.**

tenant A **tenant** pays money to live in an apartment or house.

tender   A person who is very **kind and gentle** is **tender.**
Sally is tender when she is with Linus.

Sometimes when we have hurt ourselves, we say, "Don't touch me there.   It is **tender."**   We mean that even a gentle touch may hurt us or cause us pain.

---

tennis   **Tennis** is a game played by two or four people.   You hit a ball across a net with a special bat called a tennis racket.

---

tent   In the summer, the Peanuts bunch goes to camp.   They live in the woods in **tents.**

A **tent** looks like a little house made of cloth.   A tent is easy to put up anywhere in the summer and can be rolled up and stored in the winter.

Some **tents** are very big.   I saw a circus in a big tent.

---

terrible   When the two trains hit each other, there was a **terrible** wreck.   It **made everyone afraid.**

---

test   The teacher gave the kids a **test.**   She asked them questions and they had to tell her the right answers.   If they can give her the right answers, they are happy; they have learned what the teacher wants them to know.

---

than      Here are three poles.   One pole is taller **than** the other two. All three poles are bigger **than** Woodstock.

417

thank When someone does something for you, you say "**Thank** you."
When someone gives you something, you say,
"Thank you."
We always **thank** people when they do nice things for us.
We write thank you letters for our Christmas gifts.

thankful Linus believes he has many things to thank God for. He is **thankful** to God for making him happy.

thanks When we say "**Thanks**," we mean "**Thank you**."
To give thanks means to say "Thank you."

Thanksgiving **Thanksgiving** Day comes in the month of November. Thanksgiving is a **holiday** when we give thanks for many good things.

that This is my book, and **that** is your book.
Do you see **that** tree across the street?

Lucy said **that** she wanted to go home.

the   I don't want just a dog.   I want **the** dog we saw in the store. **The** dog we saw was brown with white spots.   The other dogs were not as nice as the brown one.

---

theater   A **theater** is a building or large room in which we see movies or plays.

---

their   Father and I went to the Joneses' farm.
We went to see **their** horses.
We went to see the horses **that belong to them.**

---

theirs   My sister and I play with Lucy and her brother Linus.
These toys are ours, and the other toys are **theirs.**
These toys are ours, and the other toys **belong to them.**

---

them   Your toys are new.   Take care of **them.**   You will want to play with those toys for a long time.

---

themselves   The boys **themselves** said we should not go.
The boys did not need anyone to tell them not to go. They said it on their own.

Sally and Linus were playing by **themselves** away from the others.
Sally and Linus were playing **alone** away from the others.

then   When Mother calls, **then** I will go home.
When Mother calls, **at that time** I will go home.

First we will go to the movies.   **Then** we will have some
   ice cream.
First we will go to the movies.   **Afterward** we will have
   some ice cream.

---

there   You sit **there** while I go into the store.
You sit **in that place** while I go into the store.

I like to go to the park.   Have you ever been **there?**
Have you ever been **to that place?**

There were six candles on my birthday cake.

When I hurt myself, Mother says, **"There, there,** I'll kiss
   it and make it well."

---

they      Lucy and Linus are at the window.
   They are watching the rain.

The dogs have not eaten today,
   so **they** are hungry.
Schroeder and Roy have been
   running, so they are very hot.

Mother said, **"They** say we're going to have a hot summer."
Mother said, **"People** say we're going to have a hot summer."

thick   This wall is **thick**.
This wall is **not thin**.

The grass is tall and **thick** in the meadow.
The grass is tall and **growing close together** in the meadow.

---

thief   A person who steals is a **thief**.

  thieves   Several **thieves** stole the money, but just one thief
was caught.

---

thimble   I put a **thimble** over the end of my finger when I sew.
I push the needle with that finger.   The thimble
keeps the needle from sticking my finger.   It is made
of metal and covers the tip of my finger.

---

thin   A piece of paper is **thin**.   A wall is thick.

The grass was **thin** on the side of the hill.
The grass was **growing far apart** on the side of the hill.

The dog is **thin**.   His bones show under his skin.
The pig is fat.   He is round and heavy.

---

thing   "What's that **thing** you have there?" asked Charlie Brown.
"It's an empty basket," said Snoopy.

What are these **things?**
They are my toys.

Your **things** are all over the floor.
Your clothes and books and toys
and papers are all over the
floor.

think I **think** with my mind.   I must **think** about what to
give my mother for Christmas.

I **think** I know where Snoopy is hiding.
I **believe** I know where Snoopy is hiding.

I **thought** of a story that my grandmother used to tell me.

third Charlie Brown is
third in line.
To be third is to be the
number three.
One of his friends is
first in line.
She is number one
on the line.
The girl behind her is second.
She is number two in the line.

thirsty Peppermint Patty was very **thirsty**.
Her mouth felt dry.   When she came upon the water
fountain, she drank and drank.

thirty There are **thirty** days in September.
There are **30** days in September.

this That apple is yours, but **this** one is mine.
My brother will be six years old **this** week.
This man is my father.

thorn A **thorn** is a **short, sharp point** that grows on a plant.
There are many thorns on a rose bush.

thorough Frieda has to give her room a **thorough** cleaning.
She has to clean everything in her room,
with great care.

those   That is his toy, but **those** toys are mine.
Do you see **those** children over there?   They are having
a party.

---

though   My plant will not grow, **though** I water it every day.
My plant will not grow, **even if** I water it every day.

---

thousand   Ten times one hundred is one **thousand.**
Ten times 100 is **1,000.**

Fifteen thousand people live in our town.
How many thousand people live in your town?

---

thread   Mother sews her dress with **thread.**   She uses
cotton thread in her needle.   Thread is like
string, but is very thin.

Can you **thread** the needle?
Can you **put thread through** the needle?

---

threat   A **threat** is a **warning** that
someone plans to hurt someone
else.   When Lucy rushes
up to Linus and shouts,
"You do it, Linus, or you'll
be sorry," that's a threat.

threaten　Lucy must learn not to **threaten** people.　She must learn not to make threats.　She must learn not to try to frighten people into doing things her way.　Do you think Lucy will ever stop **threatening** the other kids?

---

three　Charlie Brown, Linus and Thibault are playing hockey.
The **three** of them are playing together.

Three is the number that comes after 2.　Let's count to **3**:
1　2　**3**.

---

thrifty　Franklin is **thrifty**.　He **saves the money** his mother gives him.　He doesn't spend it on candy.　He is **careful with money;** he says he will be thrifty and will save enough to buy new ice skates.

---

throat　My **throat** is the front of my neck.　The inside of my neck is also called my throat.　A sore throat is a throat that hurts.

---

through　Dad made a hole **through** a penny so that I could put a string in it.
Dad made a hole **from one side to the other side** of a penny so that I could put a string in it.

I read **through** the book.
I read **from beginning to end** of the book.

Frieda is **through** with her work.
Frieda has **finished** with her work.

throw

Charlie Brown is ready to
throw the ball.

He **throws** it to Snoopy.
He **tosses** it straight and high.

He **threw** it too far.
Poor Charlie Brown has not **thrown** the ball right all day.

---

thumb

Charlie Brown hurt his **thumb**
opening a can of dog food.
The thumb is the thickest
finger on each hand.
Your fingers bend in two places.
Your thumbs bend in only
one place.

---

thunder It is going to storm, and I hear a very loud noise
from the sky. That is **thunder.** Lightning and
thunder often come when we have a rain storm.

Thursday The **fifth day** of the week is **Thursday.**

tick   The **sound** made by a watch or clock is called a **tick**. Charlie Brown dropped his watch.   When he picked it up, he heard it **ticking**.   "My watch is still working," Charlie Brown said.

ticket

Charlie Brown and his friends are having a show. To see it, you must buy a **ticket**.   You must give this **small card** to someone at the door so you can go into the theater.

You also need a ticket to travel on a train, plane or ship. Your ticket shows that you have paid your fare.

tickle   Snoopy likes to have Linus **tickle** his nose.   His nose gets a funny feeling when someone scratches it very gently.   It makes him want to laugh.

That story **tickles** me.
That story **makes me laugh.**

427

tidy   Schroeder keeps his room **tidy.**   The room is **clean,** and
everything is where it should be.

Schroeder doesn't leave his clothes on the floor and his music
books all over his bed.   He always **tidies** things up.

---

tie      Snoopy is wearing a **tie** around his neck.
Daddy wears a tie with his shirt.
Their **ties** are made of silk.

The race was a **tie.**   The boys came to
the end at the same time.   Neither won.

When we **tie** a string to a kite, we **connect** the string
to the kite.   We **make a knot** in the string so that the
string and kite will stay joined.

The cowboy **tied** the horse to the fence.
Violet is **tying** a ribbon in her hair.

---

tiger   A **tiger** is a large **wild animal.**   You may see a tiger in the
zoo or at the circus.

---

tight      Linus's shoes are too **tight.**
They are **too small** for his feet.
They make his feet hurt.

Mother held me **tight** when she kissed me goodbye.
Mother held me **closely** when she kissed me goodbye.

till   Mother told us we could play outdoors **till** it was dark.
Mother told us we could play outdoors **up to the time**
it was dark.

Till means the same as **until.**

time   Lucy is looking at the clock to see what **time** it is.
It is a minute before four o'clock.

A minute is a short time.   A year is a long time.

Eight o'clock is Lucy's bedtime.

I had a good time at the party.

We had to run to be in time for school.
We had to run so that we wouldn't be late.

tin

Snoopy has found an old **tin** can that once held food.
Tin is a **metal** that is often used for food cans.

---

tiny   Something **very small** is **tiny**.   The bug was so tiny that you could hardly see it.

---

tip   The **tip** of a thing is its **very end**.   The tip of the arrow is in the tree.

Don't put the glass so near the edge of the table.
It will **tip** over.
It will **fall** over.

---

tiptoe   I walked on **tiptoe** down the stairs.   I walked **on my toes** so that no one would hear me.

tire   Charlie Brown heard the sound of the **tires** on the road
and knew the bus was going without him.

Each wheel of a bus is covered by a rubber ring filled with air.
This **tire** protects the wheel and makes the bus run smoothly.

Daddy bought four new tires for our car.

---

tired   Snoopy is **tired.**   He played hard all day and now he needs
a rest.

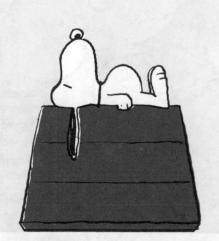

When Daddy is tired, he falls asleep in
his chair.   When I am tired, I go to bed.

431

to Go **to** the door and look out.
Go **as far as** the door and look out.

Franklin gave the cookie **to** Schroeder.

I like **to** play outdoors.   I do not like **to** stay in the house.

This is the belt **to** my blue coat.
This is the belt **that goes with** my blue coat.

---

toast Charlie Brown and his friends like to **toast** marshmallows.
To **toast** is to **brown with heat.**

They hold the marshmallows near the heat until they are brown.

Linus likes **toast** for breakfast.
Lucy is **toasting** the bread
for him in a toaster.
He likes **toasted** rolls, too.

today   **Today** is the day that is now.   Yesterday is the day before today.   Tomorrow is the day after today.

toe   We have five **toes** on each foot. We can move our toes up and down. We bend our toes when we walk.

The big **toe** is the first toe. It is useful for finding out if the water in the lake is cold.

together   Lucy and Charlie
Brown are sitting **together** on
the bench.
They are sitting **with each other**.

I sewed two pieces of cloth
together.
I sewed two pieces of cloth
to each other.

---

tomato   A **tomato** is really a **fruit,** but it tastes like a vegetable.
Have you ever eaten a ripe, red tomato right out of
the garden?   That's when **tomatoes** taste best.

---

tomorrow   The day after today is **tomorrow**.   Today is the
day that is now.   Yesterday is the day before today.

---

tongue

Linus is sticking out his
tongue.   His tongue should be
in his mouth.

We use our **tongues** to speak.
Our tongues also help us eat
and taste our food.

---

tonight   The night of today is **tonight**.   Today we do not go to
school, and tonight we are going to a movie.

too

Snoopy's collar is **too** big for him.
It is **more than** big **enough** for him.

Woodstock wishes he had a collar **too**.
He wishes he had one **also**.

tool Snoopy came to the **tool** shed to get a tool.   A tool is **something that helps us with our work**.   There are many kinds of tools.   Which tools will Snoopy need to build a new doghouse?

tooth   I have a loose **tooth** in my mouth.   Soon I will get a
            new tooth.

teeth   When I have all my **teeth,** I will be able to chew my
            food better.

---

toothbrush   Linus brushes his teeth
                 with a **toothbrush** to
                 keep them clean.

---

toothpaste   Lucy puts **toothpaste** on her toothbrush when she
                 brushes her teeth.   The toothpaste tastes
                 like candy.

---

top   Woodstock is sitting on **top** of the tree.
          He is on the **highest part** of the tree.

Put the **top**
    on the box.
Put the **cover**
    on the box.

I have a **top** that spins around and around.   It's my favorite
toy.

toss

Why would Snoopy want to **toss** his
supper dish away?
Why would he want to **throw** it away?

He is **tossing** his dish because it's empty.
He **tossed** it on the ground.

touch

"Don't **touch** this paper, Linus,"
cried Lucy.
"Don't **put a finger** on it!"

Linus **touched** it anyway.

When I walk on tiptoe, my heels don't touch the floor.
When heat touches snow, the snow melts.

toward   I am going **toward** the park.   If I keep on going
the way I am, I will get to the park.

towards   **Towards** means **toward.**

towel   When Charlie Brown takes a bath, he dries his body with a
bath **towel.**   I dry my hands on a hand
towel.   Mother dries the dishes with
a dish towel.   A towel is a piece of
cloth used to dry something.

tower   The tall, narrow part of a building is a **tower**.
Have you ever seen a church tower?

---

town   A **town** is a **small city**.   We do not live in a town.
We live in the country.

---

toy

Linus has a **toy** truck.   It is not a real truck.   It is a thing
that he plays with.

Linus and Lucy have many **toys**.   They play with their toys in
their bedroom.

---

track   A railroad **track** is the road the trains run on.
It is made of iron rails.

When an animal walks in the snow or mud, he leaves
the marks of his feet.   I saw rabbit **tracks** in the snow.

The Indians know how **to track** animals.
The Indians know how **to follow** the tracks of animals.

tractor A **tractor** is a big machine that can pull heavy things. The farmer uses his tractor to pull his plow and do other work on the farm.

trade I will **trade** books with you. I will give you my book if you will give me your book.

We **trade** with Mr. Jones.
We **buy from** Mr. Jones.

trailer I saw a car with a **trailer** on it. The trailer was like a room on wheels. People could sleep in it at night.

Some **trailers** are used to carry loads.

train A **train** is a row of railroad cars pulled by an engine.

trap A **trap** is used to catch animals. We caught a mouse in a mousetrap.

He **trapped** me into telling my secret.
He **tricked** me into telling my secret.

travel I like to **travel.**
I like to **go from one place to another.** I like to travel by airplane.

treat   Mother took us to the circus for a **treat**.   Another treat was
the lemonade and peanuts we had to eat.   A treat is
something pleasant.

I'll **treat** you to a dish of ice cream.
I'll **buy** you a dish of ice cream **for a present.**

You must always **treat** your pets well.
You must always **act** well **toward** your pets.

My aunt **treated** me like a big boy when she came to see us.

---

tree   "Look, Linus," said Charlie Brown.   "The **trees** are
beginning to bloom."

A **tree** is a **very big plant.** The tree trunk is wood. A tree has branches and leaves. There are many kinds of trees. Some are green only in summer. Some are green all the year round.

---

trick   Lucy played a **trick** on Charlie Brown.

It wasn't nice of Lucy **to trick** him.
It wasn't nice of Lucy **to fool** Charlie Brown.

My dog can do a trick.
My dog can walk on his hind legs.

---

trim   We will **trim** the Christmas tree. We will make it look pretty with lights and shiny balls and strips of silver paper.

Father can **trim** the dog's hair.
Father can **cut a little bit off** the dog's hair.

Uncle John has his hair **trimmed** every two weeks.

Mother is **trimming** my dress with white lace.
Trimming is something put on a dress to make it look prettier.

trip

Snoopy is going on a **trip.**
He is **going** someplace **away** from home.

Watch where you're going, or you will **trip.**
You'll catch your foot on something and **start to fall.**

I almost **tripped** over your suitcase.

---

trouble Kitty causes **trouble** when she pushes the sewing basket over.
Kitty causes **bother** for all of us when she pushes the sewing basket over.

If you are naughty, you may get into trouble.
Something that is not pleasant may happen to you.

trousers   He has his first pair of long **trousers**.
He has his first pair of long **pants**.

truck   Linus has a toy **truck**.   It is carrying a load of sand.
Real trucks are larger than
automobiles and are made to carry
heavy loads.

true   It is **true** that two and two are four.   It is true that the
world is round.   It is true that the sun rises in the
east.   Anything that is true is **not a lie.**

trunk   Snoopy has just arrived at camp with his **trunk**.   All his
things are packed in the trunk.   A trunk is larger
than a suitcase.

The lower part
of a tree is called
a **trunk**.   A tree
trunk is wood.

An elephant's
long nose is
called a **trunk**.

trust I **trust** you. I believe that you are honest. I believe that you will do as you say.

---

truth Always tell the **truth.**
Always tell **things that are true.**

---

try I **try** to be a good child. I will try to remember everything in my lesson. I do all I can to remember.

Why don't you try the book and see if you like it?

I **tried** to ride my bicycle down the hill, but it was too steep. Charlie Brown is **trying** to get his work done early so that he can go to the movies.

---

tub We bathe in a **bathtub.** We wash our clothes in a wash tub. The farmer sold us a tub of butter. **An open container** is a **tub.**

Tuesday **Tuesday** is the **third day** of the week.

---

tulip A **tulip** is a **flower.** It blooms in the spring.

---

tumble Baby's **tumble** off the chair made him cry.
Baby's **fall** off the chair made him cry.

When we're playing at the farm, we **tumble** in the hay.
When we're playing at the farm, we **bounce around** in the hay.

State Flag

Tennessee
The Volunteer State

During the Mexican War, Tennessee was asked to send 2,800 soldiers to fight. More than ten times as many—30,000—men volunteered giving this state its nickname. Daniel Boone and Davy Crockett both lived here, and three presidents were Tennesseans: Andrew Jackson, Andrew Johnson and James K. Polk. Today about two-thirds of the people of Tennessee are farmers, raising corn, cotton and tobacco. Many visitors come to see the beautiful Smoky Mountains in this state.

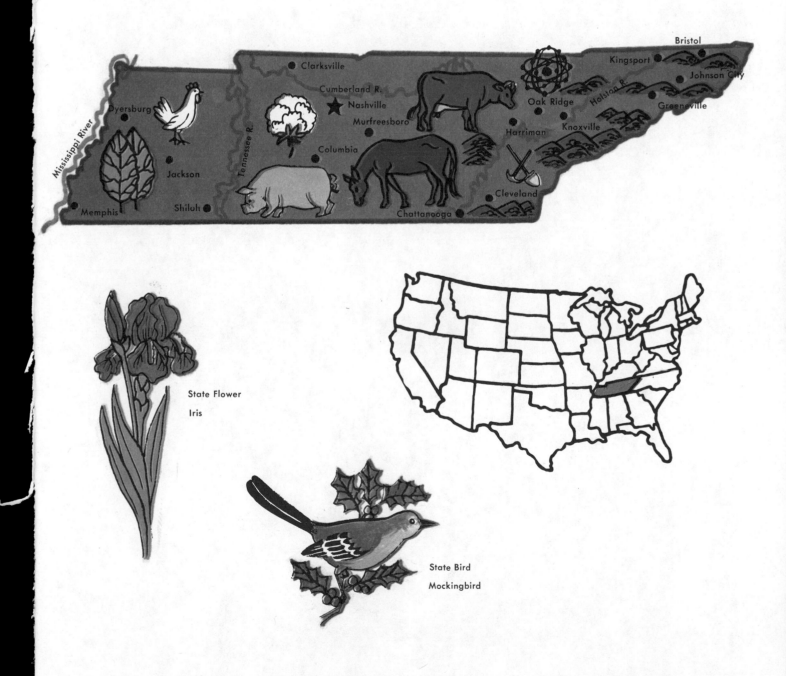

State Flower
Iris

State Bird
Mockingbird

Texas
The Lone Star State

State Flag

Many flags have flown over Texas: first the Spanish, then the French, then the Mexican, and the fourth bore the star that claimed Texas to be an independent country. After joining the United States, Texas then fought with the South in the Civil War and flew the Confederate flag. When the war ended, Texas rejoined the U.S. and for many years was proud to boast that it was by far the biggest state in the Union—until Alaska, even bigger, became our forty-ninth state.

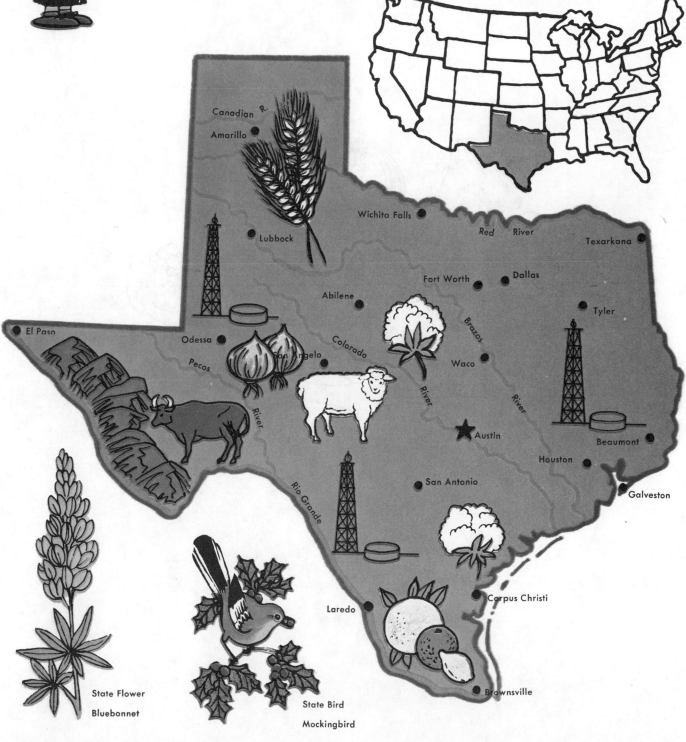

Canadian R.
Amarillo
Wichita Falls
Red River
Texarkana
Lubbock
Dallas
Fort Worth
Abilene
Tyler
El Paso
Odessa
Colorado
Brazos
Waco
Pecos
San Angelo
River
Austin
Beaumont
Houston
Rio Grande
San Antonio
Galveston
Corpus Christi
Laredo
Brownsville

State Flower
Bluebonnet

State Bird
Mockingbird